Great Instrumentals

ISBN 978-1-4950-2620-1

HAL•LEONARD®
CORPORATION
7777 W. BLUEMOUND RD. P.O. BOX 13819 MILWAUKEE, WI 53213

Visit Hal Leonard Online at
www.halleonard.com

ALLEY CAT

By FRANK BJORN

Moderately slow

BATMAN THEME

Words and Music by
NEAL HEFTI

Bat Rock tempo

9

BEATNIK FLY

Words and Music by IRA MACK
and TOM KING

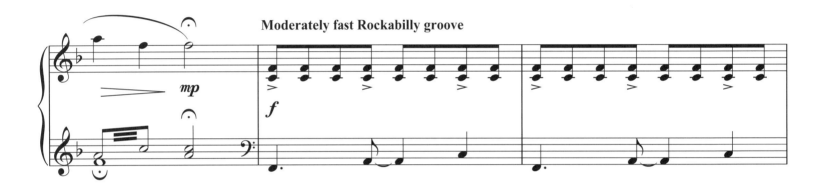

To Coda ⊕

CISSY STRUT

By ARTHUR NEVILLE,
LEO NOCENTELLI, GEORGE PORTER
and JOSEPH MODELISTE, JR.

Medium Funk

CLASSICAL GAS

Music by MASON WILLIAMS

D.S. al Coda
(take 2nd ending)

CODA

FEELS SO GOOD

By CHUCK MANGIONE

In a bright 2

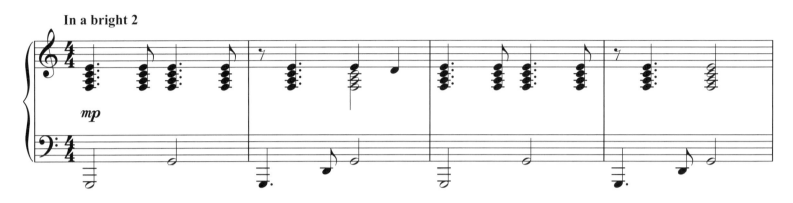

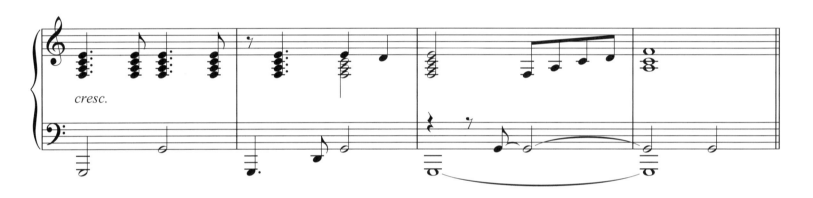

CODA

GREEN ONIONS

Written by AL JACKSON, JR., LEWIS STEINBERG,
BOOKER T. JONES and STEVE CROPPER

D.S. al Coda

CODA

dim. poco a poco

HONKY TONK
(Parts 1 & 2)

Words and Music by BERISFORD "SHEP" SHEPHERD,
CLIFFORD SCOTT, BILL DOGGETT
and BILLY BUTLER

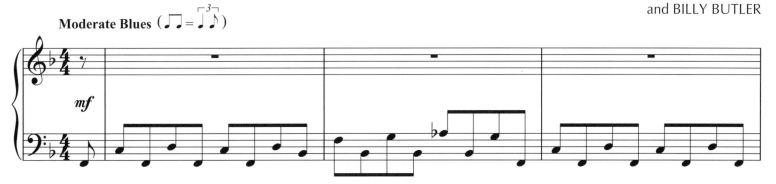

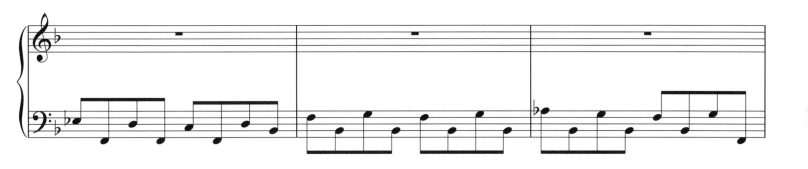

THE HAPPY ORGAN

By KEN WOOD,
DAVID CLOWNEY and JAMES KRIEGSMANN

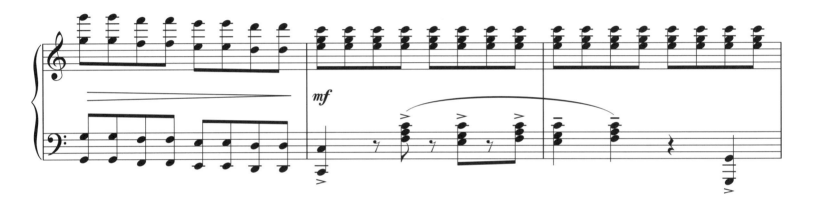

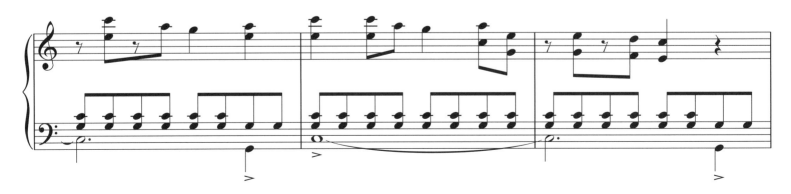

HAWAII FIVE-O THEME

from the Television Series

By MORT STEVENS

With a driving beat

LAST DATE

By FLOYD CRAMER

Slowly

*Play grace notes on the beat.

LOVE IS BLUE
(L'amour est bleu)

English Lyric by BRYAN BLACKBURN
Original French Lyric by PIERRE COUR
Music by ANDRE POPP

Moderately

MIDNIGHT IN MOSCOW

Based on a song by VASSILI SOLOVIEV-SEDOY
and M. MATUSOVSKY
New Music by KENNY BALL

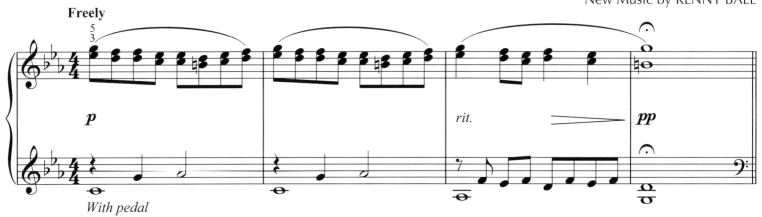

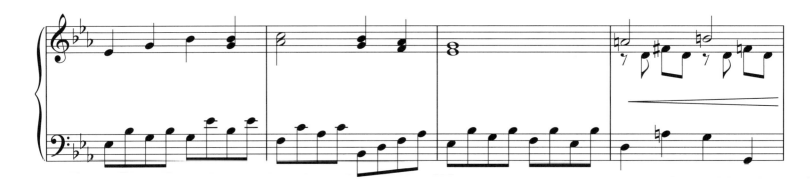

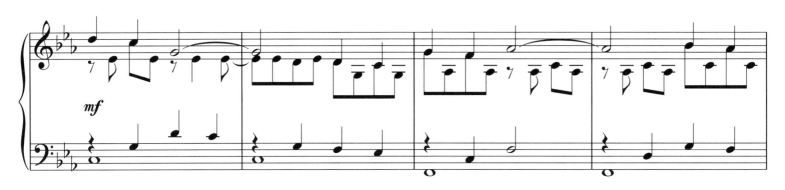

PETER GUNN
Theme Song from the Television Series

By HENRY MANCINI

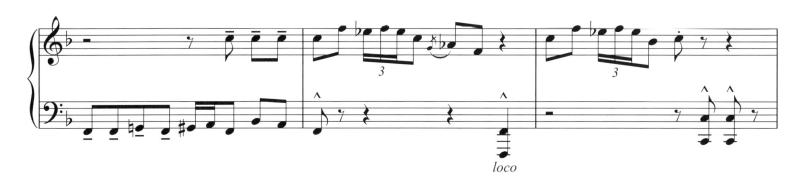

loco

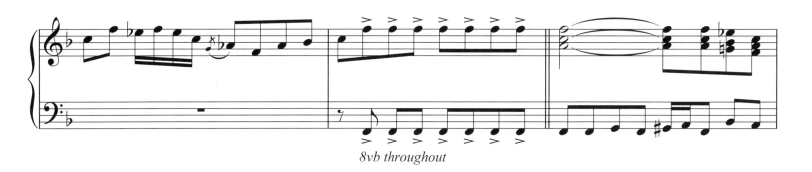

8vb throughout

MISIRLOU

Words by FRED WISE,
MILTON LEEDS, JOSÉ PINA
and SIDNEY RUSSELL
Music by NICOLAS ROUBANIS

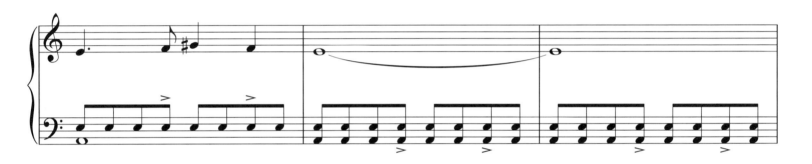

MISSION: IMPOSSIBLE THEME

from the Paramount Motion Picture MISSION: IMPOSSIBLE

By LALO SCHIFRIN

Moderate Dance beat, with drive

To Coda ⊕

THE PINK PANTHER

from THE PINK PANTHER

By HENRY MANCINI

Moderately, mysterioso

D.S. al Coda

CODA

PIPELINE

By BOB SPICKARD
and BRIAN CARMAN

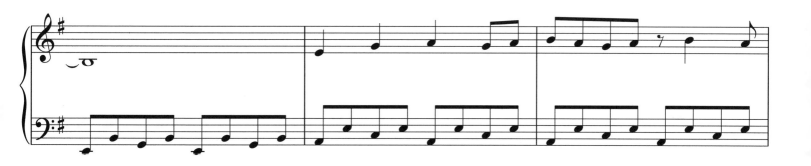

To Coda ⊕ 1.

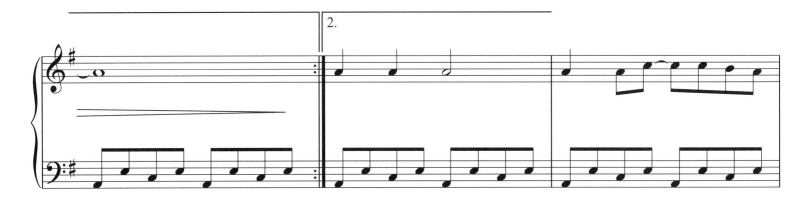

2.

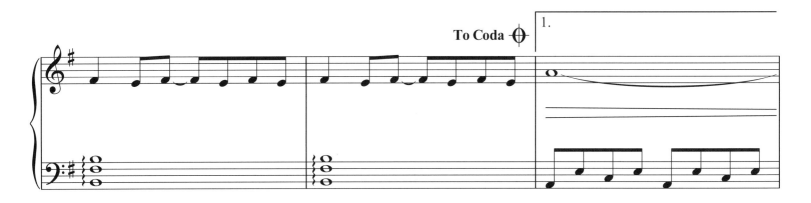

D.C. al Fine

CODA

REBEL 'ROUSER

By DUANE EDDY
and LEE HAZLEWOOD

Moderately bright

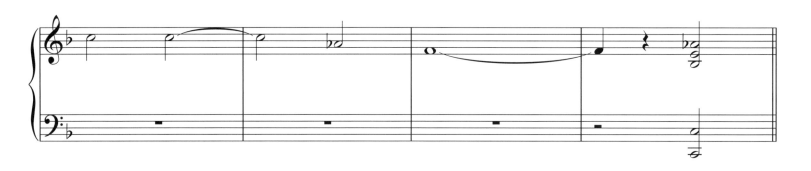

SLEEPWALK

By SANTO FARINA,
JOHN FARINA and ANN FARINA

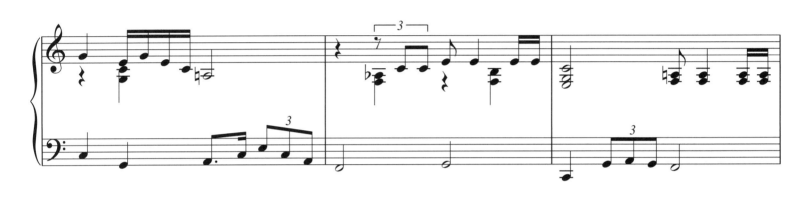

STRANGER ON THE SHORE
from FLAMINGO KID

Words by ROBERT MELLIN
Music by ACKER BILK

Moderate, relaxed feel

With pedal

THE STRIPPER
from THE STRIPPER

Music by DAVID ROSE

Blues tempo

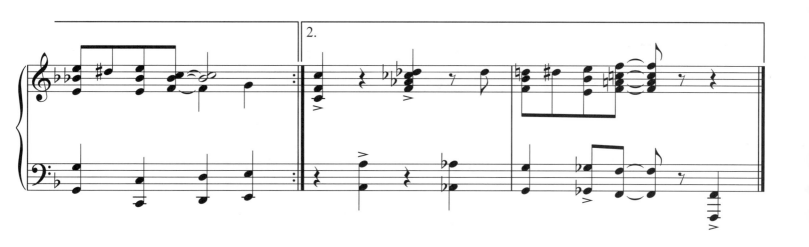

TEQUILA

By CHUCK RIO

Moderately

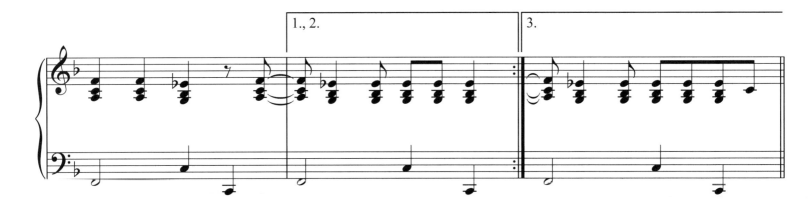

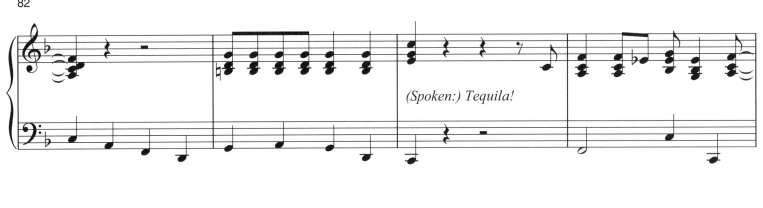

(Spoken:) Tequila!

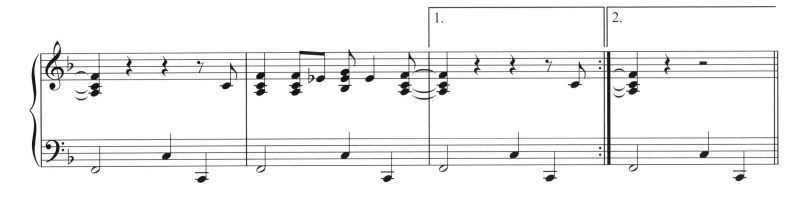

Play 3 times

(Spoken:) Tequila!

WALK DON'T RUN

By JOHNNY SMITH

WIPE OUT

By THE SURFARIS

Brightly, with a beat

To Coda ⊕

(Improvisation)

YOUR FAVORITE MUSIC
ARRANGED FOR PIANO SOLO

ADELE FOR PIANO SOLO
This collection features 10 Adele favorites beautifully arranged for piano solo, including: Chasing Pavements • Rolling in the Deep • Set Fire to the Rain • Someone like You • Turning Tables • and more.
00307585 ....$12.99

BATTLESTAR GALACTICA
by Bear McCreary
For this special collection, McCreary himself has translated the acclaimed orchestral score into fantastic solo piano arrangements at the intermediate to advanced level. Includes 19 selections in all, and as a bonus, simplified versions of "Roslin and Adama" and "Wander My Friends." Contains a note from McCreary, as well as a biography.
00313530 ....$16.99

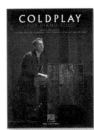

COLDPLAY FOR PIANO SOLO
Stellar solo arrangements of a dozen smash hits from Coldplay: Clocks • Fix You • In My Place • Lost! • Paradise • The Scientist • Speed of Sound • Trouble • Up in Flames • Viva La Vida • What If • Yellow.
00307637 ....$14.99

DISNEY SONGS
12 Disney favorites in beautiful piano solo arrangements, including: Bella Notte (This Is the Night) • Can I Have This Dance • Feed the Birds • He's a Tramp • I'm Late • The Medallion Calls • Once Upon a Dream • A Spoonful of Sugar • That's How You Know • We're All in This Together • You Are the Music in Me • You'll Be in My Heart (Pop Version).
00313527 ....$12.99

GLEE
Super solo piano arrangements of 14 tunes featured in *Glee*: As If We Never Said Goodbye • Beautiful • Blackbird • Don't Stop Believin' • Dream On • Fix You • Hello • I Dreamed a Dream • Landslide • Rolling in the Deep • Sway • (I've Had) The Time of My Life • To Sir, With Love • Uptown Girl.
00312654 ....$14.99

GREAT PIANO SOLOS
A diverse collection of music designed to give pianists hours of enjoyment. 45 pieces, including: Adagio for Strings • Ain't Misbehavin' • Bluesette • Canon in D • Clair de Lune • Do-Re-Mi • Don't Know Why • The Entertainer • Fur Elise • Have I Told You Lately • Memory • Misty • My Heart Will Go On • My Way • Unchained Melody • Your Song • and more.
00311273 ....$14.95

GREAT THEMES FOR PIANO SOLO
Nearly 30 rich arrangements of popular themes from movies and TV shows, including: Bella's Lullaby • Chariots of Fire • Cinema Paradiso • The Godfather (Love Theme) • Hawaii Five-O Theme • Theme from "Jaws" • Theme from "Jurassic Park" • Linus and Lucy • The Pink Panther • Twilight Zone Main Title • and more.
00312102 ....$14.99

THE HUNGER GAMES
Music by James Newton Howard
Our matching folio to this book-turned-blockbuster features ten piano solo arrangements from the haunting score by James Newton Howard: Katniss Afoot • Reaping Day • The Train • Preparing the Chariots • Horn of Plenty • The Countdown • Healing Katniss • Searching for Peeta • The Cave • Returning Home.
00316688 ....$14.99

PRIDE & PREJUDICE
12 piano pieces from the 2006 Oscar-nominated film, including: Another Dance • Darcy's Letter • Georgiana • Leaving Netherfield • Liz on Top of the World • Meryton Townhall • The Secret Life of Daydreams • Stars and Butterflies • and more.
00313327 ....$14.99

GEORGE GERSHWIN –
RHAPSODY IN BLUE (ORIGINAL)
Alfred Publishing Co.
George Gershwin's own piano solo arrangement of his classic contemporary masterpiece for piano and orchestra. This masterful measure-for-measure two-hand adaptation of the complete modern concerto for piano and orchestra incorporates all orchestral parts and piano passages into two staves while retaining the clarity, sonority, and brilliance of the original.
00321589 ....$16.99

TAYLOR SWIFT FOR PIANO SOLO
Easy arrangements of 15 of Taylor's biggest hits: Back to December • Fearless • Fifteen • Love Story • Mean • Mine • Our Song • Picture to Burn • Should've Said No • Sparks Fly • Speak Now • The Story of Us • Teardrops on My Guitar • White Horse • You Belong with Me.
00307375 ....$16.99

TWILIGHT – THE SCORE
by Carter Burwell
Here are piano solo arrangements of music Burwell composed for this film, including the achingly beautiful "Bella's Lullaby" and ten more pieces: Dinner with His Family • Edward at Her Bed • I Dreamt of Edward • I Would Be the Meal • Phascination Phase • Stuck Here like Mom • Tracking • Who Are They? • and more.
00313440 ....$14.99

UP
Music by Michael Giacchino
Piano solo arrangements of 13 pieces from Pixar's mammoth animated hit: Carl Goes Up • It's Just a House • Kevin Beak'n • Married Life • Memories Can Weigh You Down • The Nickel Tour • Paradise Found • The Small Mailman Returns • The Spirit of Adventure • Stuff We Did • We're in the Club Now • and more, plus a special section of full-color artwork from the film!
00313471 ....$14.99

Prices, content, and availability subject to change without notice.
Disney characters and artwork © Disney Enterprises, Inc.

HAL•LEONARD®
CORPORATION

7777 W. BLUEMOUND RD. P.O. BOX 13819 MILWAUKEE, WI 53213

www.halleonard.com

0714